Drifting from the Bright

John Egan

Drifting from the Bright

New and selected poems

'Dark with excessive bright.' John Milton

For my wife, Marilyn

Drifting from the Bright: New and selected poems
ISBN 978 1 76109 519 1
Copyright © text John Egan 2023
Cover image: Domenico M from Pexels

First published 2023 by
GINNINDERRA PRESS
PO Box 3461 Port Adelaide 5015
www.ginninderrapress.com.au

Contents

New Poems
- Lakes and Harbours — 11
- Harmony — 13
- Looking For Significance — 14
- Monsters and Shadows — 15
- Wind and Waves — 16
- Dark Angel — 18
- Edges — 19
- Missing — 20
- Full Moon — 21
- Occasional Showers — 22
- Harbour Beach — 24
- Stunning — 25
- The Harbour — 26
- Beautiful — 27
- Three Tanka — 28
- Soft Rain — 29
- Healing — 30
- Moonlight on Metal — 31
- Stained Glass — 32
- The Revolution — 33
- Children — 34
- La Niña — 36
- Clearing Rain — 37
- Library Window — 38
- North-west Approach — 39
- Thinking of You — 40
- Facing Winter — 42
- Don't Judge a Book By… — 43
- Issue Three — 44

A Stranger	46
Aware	47
Meandering River	48
The Boss	49
Election 2022	50
Wrestle the Wind	51
Moons of Jupiter	52
Out of Darkness	54

Selected Poems

Sunlight and Violins	57
Downharbour	59
In Her Care	60
McKenzie's Farm, 1885	61
Winter's Child	62
A Journey Home	63
Speak Body, Speak Mind	64
Smoke at Midday	66
Angels in the Mind	67
Look Below the Surface	69
On Lines by Clive James	71
Central Railway, 8 a.m.	72
Neil Young Sings 'Like a Hurricane'	74
Putting to Sea	76
The Kiss	78
Greyworld	79
Railway Square	80
Werewolf	82
Outward Bound the Moon	83
Cello Concerto	84
The Graveyard Watch	85
Iron Cove	86

Effects of Fog	87
Barangaroo	89
Macdonaldtown Station, 7 p.m.	90
An Old Photo	93
The Red Hat	94
I'd Never Worked With Glamour	96
Forty Years Ago	98
Camperdown Park	100
For You	101
About a Song	102
Not Forgotten	104
Full Moon at Terrigal	105
Essence	107
On the Edge	108
Fire at Sea	109
Swans	111
There's No Script	112
Dance of the Knights	113
Water at Your Feet	114
The Lost Child	116
Talking to Winter	117
Slow Train Coming	118
Three Studies for the Temeraire	119
Broadway in the Rain	120
A Whitby Bark	122
Faces	123
And Sunrise Brings	124
Morning Steam	126
The Way to Work	127
The Song	128
So long, Marianne	129
The Owl	131

The Road	132
At the National Maritime Museum	133
Broadway to Balfour Street	134
Liminal	136
Whatever Remains	138
Acknowledgements	139

New Poems

Lakes and Harbours

Ferries nudge the Quay,
point their noses away from the harbour
as if watching the land, eager for
their passengers. A quiet ship
Fairlight, alive, her radar beacon
spins in fast motion, alert and ready.
She glides away, turns gently,
diminishes against the high-rise
at Kirribilli and is lost
around Bennelong Point, her journery
down-harbour to Manly.

The city drops behind, a jagged forest
of steel and glass. Rounding Bradley's
she cuts into the chop, dips and heaves
but keeps her feet past green headlands
and sandstone cliffs, where Middle Harbour
slides away and the sea and harbour merge,
North Head a fortress against the blue
and the horizon like another world.

More high-rises, Manly and the wooded hill
of Dobroyd Point, small boats moored off
the harbour beach like white, sleeping dogs,
tethered, waiting to be coaxed into life
but everyone is on the beach.

People swimming, wading, playing games,
children and mothers, the occasional father,
teenage boys, girls in bikinis
enjoy the flat, secure water,
not the waves of the surf beach across
the peninsula. This suburban beach
faces the harbour, a green wilderness
and the distant city, whose towers
poke above Middle Head. On either side
apartment blocks and streets, boatsheds and masts
the bay enclosed and intimate, a blue lake
that fades into quiet distance.

Another ferry noses out of the wharf
and gathers speed past the boats, looking for
the channel, looking for the direct run
back to the fabled city, high towers,
its destination and terminal, home.

Harmony

We sit in the café,
sip our teas,
chatter and laugh,
hold hands, smile
into each other's eyes.

I always look forward
to seeing what you'll wear.
I admire your clothes.
You admire my poems.

When it's time to go,
we take the short walk
down the hill
still holding hands

where the city streets
merge into us
and our lives
intertwine
like fingers.

Looking For Significance

I didn't know what I'd feel
revisiting the house
I'd lived in
nearly fifty years ago.

A teenager, me,
mowing the lawn –
a boy hitting tennis balls
against the wall.
Dad concreting,
digging a trench across the yard,
Mum hanging clothes on the line.

There are famous shrines
and temples, admired
for their beauty, but they've become
buildings as objects,
divorced from emotional context,
their significance lost.

The house is neat, well kept,
the garden well tended
with a new, brick front fence.
There are no ghosts.

I remember inside, of course,
its floor plan imprinted
in my mind, my room,
but what it's like now…?

I feel very little.

Monsters and Shadows

In the shadows of the mind
monsters and devils, angels, doubt.
Stress and disorder constantly mount.
You search but cannot find
tranquility of any kind.
A steady temptation just to shout
at shadows in the mind,
at monsters and devils, angels, doubt.

Be calm, avoid the urge to bind
ideas into rules no one can flout.
Courage, determination always count
in being certain, being blind
to phantom monsters, shadows in the mind,
no devils, only angels, do not doubt.

Wind and Waves

Normal for this time of year,
a morning nor'-easter,
stiffer than usual but not much.
There on the upper deck
a club that punches into your face.

Our ferry pushes down-harbour,
the chop and slap of wavelets,
then turns north-east and heaves
against the wind that rakes the deck
where there is no shelter,
takes your breath away. Hang onto
your hat, your sunglasses, your bag.
Don't stand, you'll be pushed down,
you'll be tossed, toppled, thrown sideways.

It's an inner-harbour ferry,
filling in for real ships, *Collaroy,
Freshwater, Queenscliff, Narrabeen*.
She's not up to the task.
Crossing The Heads, only the slightest
of swells, and she's tumbling
and lifting her twin hulls,
unbalanced and distressed.

It's economics. The Freshwater class,
too expensive to run, we're told, while crowds
are down – holidays and covid,
but they can handle the swells.

Fairlight is named for a hydrofoil
of the 1960s
that skimmed the waves like a dancer.
Can a ship be literally
out of its depth?

Dark Angel

Black hair, brown eyes.
I think of you,
dark angel
and I'm in
paradise.

Your smile, your laugh.
I hear your voice,
dark angel
and I'm listening
to a symphony.

Dark hair, brown eyes.
When we're apart
I think of you,
dark in my sight.
Black hair glows in the sun.

Edges

Something at the edge of light
where the pieces never fit,
broken bones that will not knit,

your vision blurred, drifting from the bright.
Your eyes uncertain, red with grit.
Something's at the edge of light,

distant images, birds in flight,
the virus, pandemic, random bits
of life, seams that do not sit
neatly, always at the edge of light.

Missing

I'm alone
and I think of you.
How many days until
I see you again,
hug you, chatter, flirt?
Not a day passes
that I don't
long for you.

Today a hole
in my life gaping
where you should be.
After so many years

I know exactly
its size and shape
and how you'd fill it,
precisely.

Full Moon

after Tu Fu – 712–770 CE

Above city towers, the moon, twice
its normal size, drifts in silence, rides

the red roofs of houses and restless
scatters gold on the wide river, silvers

our curtained windows and laughs in valleys
among the lonely mountains, sharp peaks, bright stars,

glides into my garden of eucalypts
and grevillea, a bright Boeing

after a flight across the world, relief
and radiance in coming home.

Occasional Showers

Meet at the café,
the other side
of Cleveland Street.

Being me,
I arrive early
and wait for you.

I'm thrilled
if you also
arrive early

but being you
you're usually
precisely on time.

Realising you're
there
kissing me,

sitting opposite,
taking my hand,
is like the world

rewarding me
for everything
disappointing.

I'm floating
on smiles
and conversation,

contentment in deluges,
sudden downpours,
showers of delight.

Harbour Beach

Mothers and children playing on the beach,
families wading in tranquil blue,
dogs on leashes wandering past.
Almost too perfect to be true.

Distinctive in yellow and green
ferries glide in and out, seagulls
in flocks and the curve of the path
that leads somewhere better. Who can tell?

Stunning

Stunning electric blue, your blouse,
see-through patterns over a camisole
to match, a black skirt and your jet-black hair
cascading over blue shoulders.

I couldn't resist taking a photo
but you were modest, didn't want to show
your face so turned away. I shot your back,
your shoulders and hair, all against

sizzling blue. I wanted your blouse
and your neck. Given time and privacy
I'd have posed you, a fashion model
for a glamour shoot against the restaurant's

plain interior. Both of us modest –
me lacking photographic skills,
you hiding your face, but not so modest
later when you admired your photograph.

The Harbour

The wind slaps your face.
There is spray in the air
as the harbour slides away
at fourteen knots.

After the heat and rain
headlands are overgrown and green.
The suburbs look smaller,
flatter, buildings not so obvious.

And in the blue distance
the Pacific is a lake
that encroaches, overwhelms
and goes on forever.

Beautiful

For Christmas
I gave you
a pen.

You used it
to write a card
to me.

I like pens.
I love receiving cards,
especially from you,

as if my gift
flew home
enriched

with
fine feathers
and love.

Three Tanka

The edge of hearing,
discords of thunder
this afternoon
at the crossroads
of rainstorm and calm.

Thunder and rain,
the sky iron-clad grey,
mist in the valleys,
hills hidden,
the mind numb.

A cool wind,
the beach deserted,
a lone fisherman
collects worms for bait,
harvests the sand.

Soft Rain

Gentle rain,
the leaves
glow and murmur,
the softness
and the glimmer.

Lullabies in the rain,
the mist
and gentle breezes,
choirs
and their voices.

Starlight
in your hair
reflects red roses,
the glamour
of streetlights

and the tenderness
of the night
that glows
in the silver
streets below.

Healing

You surround me like the sea,
absorb me into yourself
like the sky so I swim
and glide like a creature
in a softer element.

'Waterways rush over me'*
and I flow like a tide
into your smile, sunlight
and honey, old wounds soothed
in the harmony of your eyes.

* Grace Perry

Moonlight on Metal

Figures, like men, like animals,
stark and steel, bright in semi-dark.
loom from the lake's dry surface,
ghosts and phantoms striding on salt.

Torchlight moves in a pinprick beam,
shudders and jerks in his hands,
searches the darkness for that faint flash
of metal, of reflection, of life.

The dark side of the moon, starlight
on the Sea of Tranquillity.
The mechanics of movement, robot
explorers, arms like spiders,

in a world of dust, on Earth, a world
of dry salt, an arid seafloor
of an island lake, dissolved into
dry wind, the march of climate

and the movement of the ages
as the continent drifts northwards
over aeons where salt-lakes replace
grass and woodland. Sculptures and torchlight

where the level sands stretch away
in every direction like deserts
on the moon. Sand-dunes carved by wind
and gaunt birds on thin legs, screeching.

Stained Glass

Stained glass windows reflect sunlight
into the room. You're a priestess in black,
passive, silent, obedient
to the room's stillness, the quiet ticking

of a clock, traffic in the distance.
Look into silence, look into stillness.
Lower your eyes while I wait
mesmerised for time to reveal

secrets and mysteries, as questions
grow into interrogations, answers
into speeches that you do not make,
or at least, make only with your eyes,

that reveal worlds I knew nothing about.
Time passes, replies and revelations,
the High Priestess in a black dress,
the Empress grazed by light.

Colours subdue sunlight in the glass,
light in a temple, light in a tomb.
You are a teacher, a student,
the mistress and the muse.

The Revolution

after Olga Berggolts

We sang the simplest,
most straightforward of words, as if
they'd never been heard before.
The commonest of nouns
became noble and profound.
Air, light switch, glass
grew to be
sunlight, power and love.

We cleared
glaciers from the streets,
swept deluges from floodplains
and icebergs from our harbours.

Women in amazement
stood and stared
at the clean Earth,
at roads
dredged from water,
at houses excavated
from mud.

We were all sailors
at the masthead
after months at sea
who peered into the distance
and cried, 'Land Ho! Land Ho!'

Children

We played Hide and Seek.
I'm seventy-two, going on
seven. You're forty-eight,
going on eight.
Just the right ages
for childish games.

I searched the whole house
for you – nowhere,
thought there's only one place
you could be
and there you were,
under the bed
in the room I'd first
come into and talked
to your friend,
the last place I looked,
the first you'd thought of.

Your second turn
and I looked everywhere,
upstairs and downstairs twice,
mentally disregarded the coat rack
as being too small,
walked past it twice
forgetting you too are small
and there you were,
half suffocated but there.

Later we had tea
from a formal set of cups
and a teapot with flowers.
We disregarded
anything contemporary.
We both relived our childhoods,
disregarded our ages.
I loved that.

La Niña

The laneway is a pattern of silver,
shallow puddles shimmer with raindrops.

Green leaves glisten against grey sky
and the grass is a swollen carpet.

A river flows slightly downhill
from the central garden to the lane

and is a flood plain of wide mud
with tributaries and meanders,

a miniature Mississippi
as the rain is still falling and

an unyielding veneer wraps itself
across the sky. Raincoats and umbrellas

and the dull glow of a sun
hidden by a wet world.

Clearing Rain

after Tu Fu

Thin clouds at the edge of the sky
pushed by westerlies from far frontiers
where the sun brightens morning landscapes
no longer mired in mud and endless rain.

Riverside willows, kingfisher greens
and red pear trees beside mountain paths.
From the town walls notes of a far flute.
A lone goose climbing into empty skies.

Library Window

Light rain continues to fall,
traffic buzzes and glides
along the damp highway
and umbrellas bump in the street.

A wattle, sparsely engraved
with yellow flowers, late in the season,
stands guard over the small square
at the entrance to the Town Hall.

In the distance, tall buildings,
in the foreground the library's
rain-streaked window and a chair
inviting and snug to watch the scene.

North-west Approach

Like a gathering storm,
the first hint of hum,
building to a crescendo roar,
changing tone as it approaches.

Deepening to contralto
if two engines,
baritone if four,
then the hint of vibrato,

turbofans spooling up
as the jet passes,
fading into distance

and another takes its place
like models on a catwalk
or rock concerts in the air.

Thinking of You

When I think of you
it's always your lovely, long black hair
that comes to mind.

When I draw a card for you
it's always positive – the Empress,
the Queen of Cups, six of Wands.

When I'm with you
I'm always relaxed and happy,
full of confidence.

When you're serious
you're very serious
but there's mischief in your brown eyes

and the little girl is always
just below the surface.
She breaks out in giggles and laughter,

in tricks and jokes.
You love lollies and chocolates,
surprises and adventure,

fantasies and stories.
We play Hide and Seek,
Blind Man's Bluff, cards.

I love your wit,
your intelligence, imagination,
your empathy and your style.

When
I think of you
it's always…

Facing Winter

after Tu Fu

New ghosts populate the country.
There is war and grief-stung women.

The clouds are ragged and evening settles
into a dance of rain and sleet.

My jar is drained of wine and the stove
offers only the illusion of warmth.

There is no news and my soul is wounded
by empty words woven into the wind.

Don't Judge a Book By…

Checking the local bookshop
to see if any more
of my books were sold.

A young woman browsing
the poetry section,
an opportunity,

grabbed my book,
said to her, 'If you like poetry
this is excellent.'

She looked at me,
at my picture on the back
and we both smiled.

She looked inside,
at the front cover
and liked it.
She bought my book.

When I got home,
I looked at my book,
tried to see it

as a stranger might –
some poems, not bad –
but I really liked the cover.

Issue Three

The poetry's a higher standard
than the two previous issues –
well-written, sensitive, some dramatic,
even moving and each is worthy
of its place, but there is conformity.
Most are well-mannered in a middle-class,
Anglican sort of way, the same nature poems
that show flowers and gardens, landscapes
and rivers, where admiring feelings
are kept politely under control
and there is appreciation of
the neat environment, the tidy trees.

There is no poem that strides up to you,
grabs your collar and lifts you off your feet,
that screeches like a banshee in your ear,
that leaves you on the ground, seeing stars
collapse in a distant galaxy,
feeling the pulse of the Earth rotate
on its axis of days, or explode
into seasons so vivid they sing to you.

There is no poem that reverberates
in the grey depths of oceans, like the song
of blue whales, or vibrates as thunder
heard by dark-skinned women kneeling on beaches
among seashells in warm lagoons.

I yearn to write the poem that lifts you,
that shrieks, that throws you to the ground
and leaves you empty, struggling for breath,
that bellows like whale song into fathoms
and leagues, the poem that states with all
confidence, 'I am here and there is now
nothing else you need.'

A Stranger

after Elena Shvasts

The mirror
gazes out at me
and is mocking me
by being
so creative.

In it I see
an old man,
bent and hairless.

I've noticed mirrors
show some changes
over the years
but I've always seen
a face I knew.

I think I'd be
less startled
by some hideous ogre
than the stranger
I see there now.

Aware

Started from scratch,
ran my fingernails
down the window,
the growling of glass
under pressure

and the shivers
up and down my spine
like realising
the loyalty you'd given
was not being returned.

Meandering River

after Tu Fu

1.

Each falling blossom diminishes the spring.
Its early splendour fades into a bland summer
and we all grieve. I want to watch every flower
but I can't sustain such deep wounds. I sip my wine.

Ravens haunt the ruins along the river
and the royal tombs are inhabited by dragons
rearing as horses. I search the soul of the world
for its consequences which entangle my life.

2

I've pawned my spring clothes for wine. I sip it slowly
every day on the banks of the river.
I'm drunk. My debts are building in every tavern
but then, who lives to be eighty anyway.

Butterflies plunge deep into flowers which shimmer
in the sun. In flight, dragonflies catch fire.
The wind and the light instil insights which spread
from the river's flow into all our bloodstreams.

The Boss

Bruce Springsteen strides across the stage
microphone in hand, behind him
an army of upturned faces in awe
of his voice, mesmerised by his sheer,
'Take this song', determined presence.

He raises his arm and they explode
into the chorus of 'My Home Town',
chant the words as if drilled soldiers,
again at the pointing of an arm
a battalion of voices sings.

Again and again as if the mere
raising of arms is commander's order
to crush the individual,
to perform in unison words
about an obscure New Jersey town
where he was born. A thousand voices
compelled by magic to rise
in chorus, to sing like a nation,
to sway, arms raised, to the swing
of music like wind through a wheat field.

The signal to cut with his hands,
a command curt and precise
to press the air into silence
after a storm.

Election 2022

'Building a better future
side by side with you.'
The election approaches,
corflutes decorate every pole.
Party members hand out How-to-Vote cards
to approaching electors.
Some accept gladly, others reject them
and many just ignore them
as if their minds are made up
or they simply don't care.

The faces of the candidates
smile into the street,
all white, all middle-class,
as if they can bring
happiness and wealth
to voters disillusioned,
anxious and angry.

There is a sense of disconnection
as if everyone's seen this farce
many times already and regardless
of those elected, life will continue
much as it did before,
if not nasty, brutish and short
then irritating, confused,
tedious and in the end
shorter than it needs to be.

Wrestle the Wind

Raise your collar against the rain.
Button your coat against the wind.
Leave your corner, step into the ring
where the storm, your opponent – huge
contours wreathed in haze.

With all your strength push forwards,
grapple him, feel his cold breath sting
your face with rain, bite your balance,
stagger you with hammer blows. Lean
into his liquid spite. An armlocked wind
overpowers you, drags you, hurls you

into the ropes, twists your neck and shoulders
into his grip. Your coat is drenched, your shirt
limp with downpour and sweat, your feet
like sponges in their boots and the storm
has you, collapses you onto the mat.
Holds you down for the count – One! Two! Three!

You're trapped under his weight and out.
The storm raises his arms above you
in the lashing trees, in the cloud-black sky
and the match is lost, you've been thrown
by wind and rain, lost to the heavyweight
champion of storms.

Moons of Jupiter

Io, Ganymede, Europa
and Callisto: the Medicean Planets,
now Jupiter's Galilean moons.

Also Adrastea, Metis, Thebe,
Amalthea and seventy others.
Galileo observed them
four hundred years ago, the first moons
around any other planet.

They hurled ideas about the universe
into chaos and confusion –
heliocentric not geocentric,
the sun's gravity binds even
Jupiter, whose own gravity
holds eighty satellites, a system
too that revolves around the sun.

Io, planet of ice and fire,
a surface that bulges
under gravity and heat,
liquid crust, fountains of lava,

Ganymede, ice and rock, oxygen
in a thick atmosphere, upheavals
in the distant past. The largest moon
in the solar system, larger
than Mercury and Pluto,
almost the size of Mars.

Europa's ice, salt water below,
hydrothermic vents in its ocean floor.

Callisto's surface, the oldest
and most heavily cratered,
may also enclose water.

The largest moons of the largest planet,
each a unique world, unlike
the Earth and its own moon.
The hidden oceans of Europa
are the most likely places anywhere
in our solar system to find life.

Out of Darkness

In early winter darkness,
this small, poorly-lit side-street,
an inner suburb and the lights
of Broadway fading behind me.

I'm walking directly into night,
warehouses and brick walls guiding me
towards the warm arms of light
stretching to greet me, enfold me,

where they spill out across my path,
the welcoming door of a restaurant,
food and wine, conversation and laughter.

I'm thinking of my friend who's there
waiting at our table near the window,
my footsteps leading through the dark

and the cold towards warmth and light
where her arms will enfold me.

Selected Poems

Sunlight and Violins

I watch the midday sun
hurl yellow crescents on a web
of ripples, silver star-flowers
bursting on the harbour's
solid blue. I think again of you,
dark angel, winter escapee
toward the alien north,
your black hair burning
in the glare, thirty degrees
of hard-beat tropic sun,
a humid Darwin afternoon
and early morning flight
away from winter here.

The northern foyer
of the Concert Hall, I sit
with Olsen's midnight mural,
Slessor's *Five Bells* coldly ringing out,
its violet, purples, indigo
covered from the colour-bleaching sun
as you are hidden now
by a continent of curtain air.
It glows with a cold, submarine
reflected light that burns
intense and aqueous as your dark eyes
like starfish that sob to the moon.
I see you dressed as always in
feminine, black, romantic clothes
the angel of my winter nights,
my mannequin of stars and dreams.

Solid then, hull and bow-wave, the *Queenscliff*
erupts across my vision, beats in the glass,
slices into blue, throws the silver
into foam, sizzles into movement,
the ferry's wide, down-harbour drive
towards the dazzle and the sea
as you beat naked on the bed,
our last night together, your body
wracked by wild, wide frenzies
that snapped your inhibitions
into spasms, storms and floodwaves
breaking cleanly into throes
of flowers and stars, an ecstasy
of heat and skin.

And here with a startled
silver-blue, the real harbour
blazes in the windows just below.
I wait this afternoon for Bruch's
wild violins to lift me
into passion and to power
against the blue, the darkened
concert hall, from water
and the cold, a clear,
bright infinity of air
as you, hurtling from the morning
into Capricorn, had flown
away towards the sun.

Downharbour

Collaroy glides out of the Quay,
a sharp turn into the southern channel
and the diesels throb in the long throat
of headlands and water, where steel and wash

roll with the tides of the moon,
her pulse and her slide downharbour
along the edges of the burning sea
to the wide, wild waves of the world.

Round Bradley's Head, it's a different seascape.
The land drops away, a thin coast,
indistinct, wedding-cake beacons, the gulls
and the yachts. South Head's a wall

at the end of the charted earth
that bars her course, forces her north where jaws
of the sea threaten, as she dances to balance
the swells and troughs – she dips and she plunges and sways

like a soft rider, then sweeps on
to applause from Middle Head where she bows,
slows to drift, safe, relaxed and here,
home to the sheltered arms of cove and wharf.

In Her Care

The nurse you remember, the night before,
in Emergency, who smiled and talked,
made you feel cared-for in pain, meets you
at the end of the corridor.

You're drugged, your head tilts spinning, you're hot,
blanketed, a warm baby in dreamscapes
of fuzzed and spiralled impressions. Somehow
you're in a wheelchair. You want to sleep

not wait dangling like this, outside
the X-ray room. People keep passing.
Someone says something to you. You form
a reply. Your brain and mouth disconnect.

Lie down, turn over, do what the nurse says.
But how do you remember what that is?
She smiles, talks to you. You want to reply.
You're wheeled back to your bed, leap into sleep.

Months later, I remember the ambulance,
being wheeled into the operating theatre,
the cold in my room waiting for discharge,
but mainly the nurse, her voice, her eyes…

McKenzie's Farm, 1885

for Nellie Williams 1923–2015

From the hill above the creek, a photo
straight across the valley to Broughton Head,
sandstone remnant of the ancient plateau,
wooded with high forests. The farmhouse obscured
behind large trees, fences, cowsheds,
and all the roads were merely tracks.
The house still stands, high above the corner,
Broughton Vale and Boundary Roads. The fence,

the farm, the trees, vanished. The house
almost derelict. Nellie lived there forty years.
She, the white-haired angel of the valley,

who died there at ninety-two. What it was before
no one thought or knew. Always Nellie's house,
always. The plaque now reads 'Nellie's Corner'.

Winter's Child

Born in Cancer, sign of the crab,
the middle of the darkest winter –
coal strikes and power blackouts,
industrial turmoil, the cold –
born in a distant suburb, months premature,
the outskirts of the city, worlds away
from my parent's home, unexpected arrival.
There was nowhere else for my mother to go.
The doctors gave my father no hope
for my survival. Small and sick, malformed,
wrapped in a blanket, a knitted beanie,
fed but otherwise abandoned.

I've felt impervious to cold, comfortable
at deepest midnight, obsessed by sub-zero,
snow and ice, but July
was always the worst of months,
cruel viruses that held me down for weeks,
writhing in an insane bed.
Anxious for the spring and for September,
the new sign of Virgo, the month
I should have been born.

Born in Cancer, sign of the crab, hardy on land,
hardy in the sea and in the mud between.
A child of winter, still struggling
to make peace with the cold, still learning
to consider all the seasons crabwise,
from all directions, light and dark,
the sun and the moon, the sea.

A Journey Home

The small diesel train buzzes down
from Kiama, passengers queue
at the doors, wait as the platform
slides beside their feet and they step out.
The train has skirted the hills and coast
where ridges collapse into the sea,
has burrowed through tunnels under cliffs
and wheeled past scenic bays and beaches.

Whistled and hummed on its long search
for easier gradients
south of Gerringong, scurried along
the fertile Beach Road, flat and fast,
to Berry, where the rounded hills
encroach the Shoalhaven's floodplain

Pedestrians walk with purpose
to familiar shops where they're met by
the usual faces. They buy
the usual things, stand and chat, or not.
The streets are quiet this early afternoon
as I drive out along the river road
that leads inland to the same waiting hills.
I take the small winding road,

drive through foothills, across the creek,
where it meanders among downslopes
and twists around the feet of ridges
to the end of the long valley
and the final steep grades homewards
under the sheer, black, familiar cliffs.

Speak Body, Speak Mind

for Stephen Phillips

The body speaks to the brain,
'I'm hurt, be depressed'
or 'I feel good, laugh.'

The mind speaks to the body,
'I don't like this, stomach
get sick', or
'That's beautiful,
generate energy, run.'

When there's stress
communication stutters.
If you fall
your mind's numb
but every muscle seizes
to protect itself
and stays seized
until it feels safe enough
to relax again.

Some hurts are so deep
the brain doesn't know they've happened.
The trauma of birth,
the trauma suffered as a baby
recurs, years later.
You don't know why.

Never bonded with my mother,
I now realise, nor
she with me.
Born months premature,
separated at birth, Mum
to another hospital
to recover, me,
fed but otherwise abandoned.
The doctors said,
'There's no hope. He won't survive.'

Every year
around my birthday,
I'm flattened by any virus
floating by, a low period.

Is it my brain saying,
'It's that time again, get sick,'
or my body saying,
'This new thing, life, is too hard,
just give up.'

Smoke at Midday

Sydney, 10 December 2019

Lavender Bay and the towers of Milsons Point,
curves of arch and the precise pylons of the bridge,
a view I've enjoyed for years, as my friends
read their poetry. In sunlight and in rain,
the sharp edges of buildings clarify
the exact sky, the world defined in windows.

Today a grey seepage, air glued by smokehaze,
tangible as flannel, choking the bay
like coalstack exhaust, thick and heavy.
Over an hour, I watch as the bridge disappears.
Vague at first, a charcoal abstract, its lines
dissolve into imprecise, eaten away, gone.

The buildings across the bay slowly vanish.
Smoke deletes them, their mass and bulk erased.
Even the closer buildings smudged. Beyond them
blankness, flat as a grey-painted wall.

For the first time, I hear foghorns
on the harbour, as ferries clutch blindness
and grope along paths into a zero made tangible,
their sirens howling in distress. It's only midday
as the harbour merges with the sky and both
close down into nothing visible at all.

Angels in the Mind

'…we need to acknowledge
visitations by intense psychological
presences, and that birds are the
closest things we have, more or less,
to angels.' – Robert Adamson

On the balcony watching lorikeets
shrapnel into splintered colours, prisms and
explosions of rainbow, I thought of you
dark angel, Spanish eyes, your nightfall hair
and patient gaze unwavering, direct
in the power of silence, your being
exactly who you are and knowing it,
as shadows know the night, though intimate
with sunlight ignore it, irrelevant and false.

Then suddenly a cacophony of wings, a blast
of cascade air and two huge messengers
in their power and purity all white
like daylight angels dropped from heaven –
two perfect sulphur-crested cockatoos
trailing glamour through a summer afternoon, shrill
as a bride, her train and gown of gorgeous wings,
groomed and radiant. I glimpsed the elegance
in symmetry of nature and the mind:

dark angels haunt reality like ghosts.
Those more blatant voyagers hurled like songs
down from the dazzled sky, colour and light,
enchantments by the obvious and loud,
or the permanence of the old shadows,
still and silent chronicles swept by night,
angels from unseen edges of the moon,
the simplicity of a dream, darker
presences, poised in mansions of the mind.

Look Below the Surface

My father was awed by style and glamour –
working class boy, the excesses of wealth
etched in his brain, 'a little bit of swish',
five-star hotels, expensive cars,
tailored suits. It was only in his senior years
he could afford any of these.

His eldest son, never impressed
by ostentation, I didn't need
luxury or to draw attention
to myself, responded to real beauty:
Manet's paintings, Beethoven's symphonies,
the poetry of Yeats, always realised
the dilemma of the superficial:
the impressive and desirable
can hide tawdry reality.

Twelve years wasted teaching in a school
whose main ethic was surface morality,
nine in another run by a
psychopath, where nothing mattered
so long as he looked good. I guess the kids
were educated somehow but I still
worry if they survived the surface sheen,
the mere appearance of good.

Rarely viewed the world from the same angle
as others, always looked below the skin,
but that has made me cynical perhaps.
I wonder what Dad would think now,
would he quietly take me aside
and show me how the world looked to someone
born in the '20s, who lost his father
to the effects of gas, who grew up
in the Depression and flew bombing missions
against the Japanese at an age
I was still at university,
who struggled to start a career and raise
a family in the not-so-golden 1950s.

Or would he be wise enough to see the fake,
ignore the superficial, or just laugh
at me, the whole glamorous, modern world
and enjoy the circus of the corrupt.

On Lines by Clive James

'All is not lost, despite the quietness
that comes like nightfall now.' From a distance
the hum of traffic, the constant buzz

of a city attending to its own
immediate business. In this room
no sounds disturb a mild mid-afternoon.

Cascades of thoughts and feelings merged
with memory, stars rising from the darkest
recesses of space and time. They occupy

larger shares of now than they've ever been
entitled to. They bully themselves into
quiet places, bustle with their elbows

and fists towards the shadows, squat like toads
in rooms and corridors. And yet silence
generates new courage from old defeats,

surges with strategies conceived by night,
designs to throttle the endless cycles
of disappointment, build the strength to seize

bullies by the throat, grapple them away,
and carve the coming day into patterns
fecund with the morning and its light.

Central Railway, 8 a.m.

The concourse throbs, movement and rush.
Crowds ebb and swell, the sigh and hiss of trains.
They shimmer in like mannequins
trailing slinky, silver gowns.
At every platform's end they stop, pretend demure,
survey the catwalk's audience
with blue and yellow lipsticked faces
and bored with this so ordinary fashion,
they pout for yet another curtain call.

Electronic gates buzz and thump
in time to tickets and the stomp
of morning travellers, their time and push.
Commuters walk or run or shuffle
past the glass walls and the latticework
of iron, marble floors and brown-bricked walls,
the sharp-haunched, crenellated stone
of archways, all the permanence of steel,
the early years a previous century,
its dignity and masonry and power.
The squalor, sleaze and raunch of blatant
BUY ME NOW contemporary commerce
and its selling blitz with all the colours
of crass, loud with signs and competition –
Station Manager, Newslink, Bakehouse,
Grand Central Bar and Bistro, Hungry Jack's…

Departure boards in rows. The station clock.

Anxious, wary travellers
fidget ports and bags, hoist their backpacks.
Others linger and wait for later trains
but daily workers dash away
to Eddy Avenue, their transit buses,
the suburbs east and south, or hurry through
marble arches into Railway Square
or catch the light rail on to Chinatown.

Monday morning 8 a.m.,
my only coffee of the day.
I sit and watch and listen,
breakfast cups and plates, the coo of chatter,
the pigeons' clear-cut monologue
and creaking flush of wings in flight,
arrivals, departures and the sometimes
lateness of their running times,
an overnight express from Melbourne,
slow trains from the Central Coast.
The great iron roof. The working week.

Neil Young Sings 'Like a Hurricane'

Wind and rain
massing on the horizon,
the organ's groundswell.
In the eye of the storm
guitars pulse like heartbeat.

The song's a missile vibrates
on its launching pad,
any minute might explode
into orbit, unleash itself
from bonds of reason and control.

The song's a locomotive
mad with steam,
brakes still on
but runaway's a juggernaut,
hurled planet
across the world.

The song builds to chaos,
slow crescendos like the wind,
listeners driven by
dark storms of organ and guitar.

Ride the tempest, be the sky's mage,
or bury yourself deep under stone,
while the whirlwind chords rush past,
shelter from the song's onslaught,
feel its blast.

I watched your tranquil face dissolve,
distorted, wild with rage.

Towns are derelict,
trees are smashed,
the mountain streams are torrents
and the golden beaches gone
but all you did
was turn your back
and calmly walk away.

You are like the hurricane
that rages through the night.
In concentric rings of fury
the singer finds his calm
only in your eyes.

Putting to Sea

In any voyage of consequence,
though imprecise in time and space,
there is an image of a thin line,
somewhere between past and future,
between harbour and the open sea,
that once crossed…

Stop now, among the frantic hauling
of sheets and blocks,
look now, beyond the helmsman's
dark, obsessive stare,
through intricacies
of yard and line and sail,
beyond the lurching taffrail,
to where the ship's frail track
is a chaos
of wind and current
and there is no coast.

Here your commitment narrows
to only this:
drive your own ship
with all the mechanism
of screeching winches
and shifting forms of those
who seem as friends,
who seem intent as you
to sweat and bully her headlong
to whatever lies beyond
the last thin line
of dark horizon.

From the cliffs
near Queenstown, Ireland,
one image remains –
like a child's toy
a distant ship
steams into an immensity of sea,
towards an implacable
grey, horizon.

One final image.
A formal photo
of a man with glasses
and fair hair,
in an academic gown,
who looks strangely
past the camera
with a light, impassive stare.
My self at twenty-nine.

Look now
through the intricacies
of life and work and love;
at fifty-four
there is no frail track to the past
and in all the chaos
of wind and current,
there is no coast at all.

The Kiss

You opened the door
and I shattered into slivers
of joy.

Fragments glowed with laughter,
led me shimmering
like stained glass
into the Sainte-Chapelle
of your room

and when I held you
I was golden as sunlight
and when we kissed
you were silver in moonlight
and the air between us
broke into diamonds,
scattered shards in prisms

and a Versailles of mirrors
reflected a radiance
of glass and jewels and love.

Greyworld

Outside the train, a doubtful world.
Mist dissolves reality, grey vistas,
damp aromas outside this thin cocoon
of artificial light, my dreams disturbed

only by the guard's announcement –
'Next stop, Katoomba,' and here I step out
where a sudden platform, like a stage set,
slides from the mist into the solid world.

Damp wisps cling to my face, moist veils,
spidery and soft, and my uncertain
confrontation with slippery exits
to shadowlands of brickwork and greyworld.

In the street, a ghost town of shapeless forms,
shop windows, cafés alight in mistglow,
buildings floating like dreadnoughts, but sinking
away downhill into a mist-haunted ocean.

Railway Square

Pedestrians throb
in tune to the beating
of buses
and the brakes of cars.

Traffic lights
switch from yellow
to red
like a pulse.

Advertisements splatter
like stains of blood
on doorways split by music
and by noise,
command respect
because they're huge
and red.

Railway tunnels
are hot,
the channelled arteries
of crowds aware
of guitars and cash
their songs warm
merely with the words
of love.

Major roads cross here
like the four chambers
of the heart,
like long legs
under the short, tight skirts
of buildings.
Their knees press
modestly together,
thighs like roofs
of bus shelters in glass
and silver.

Women in business suits
checking the data,
adjusting the pace
as morning filters
into longer hours,
the bloodstream crowds thinning.
Buskers count their coins
and walk away,
less music
and quieter songs.

Buses on Broadway
driving south
are leaving the heart.

Werewolf

A full moon
perfumes your dreams.

In your room
too much light
and no reflection
in any mirror.

Your bed is a spoiled page.
No place to lie, no pen
to lie with.

The door opens onto stairs
and the stairs lead to doors.
Beyond is the street,
a row of lit terraces
shadows exit.

The moon
leans against walls and screams.

Railway yards and empty tracks
point into other suburbs
and you nose magnetic streets
until there are no suburbs
and the high, white skeletons
of eucalypts cradle the moon
in towers of bells and the air
just keeps ringing.

Outward Bound the Moon

The moon and its face
and its smiling
enticed you to the road.
Eyes incited by moonlight
travelled beyond goodbyes
and tempted the future
in breathing.
Hungered by weavers of words,
you swallowed their verses and lies.

Where are the promises
made to the moon?
Still incessant and breaking in waves,
they're swept like breath to the sea
and the words that blossomed between us
wavered away like sighs
and the tracks of ships
beating outward
and islands that burn to the moon.

Cello Concerto

From the belly
of the cello
rings the great requiem
for all those millions dead

and Elgar's
yearning theme
for the years
before 1914.

A rolling adagio
of hills and valleys
for the green lands
and the lost.

The plaintive sob,
the pain
for what the century
could have been
but never was.

The song
of Verdun, Passchendaele
and the Somme,
the raising up of flags
and in cold trenches
the cutting down of lives.

The Graveyard Watch

From midnight to four, spirits
of drowned sailors rise to surface
in a mist that clings to the sea,
in a white sheen of ice or bones,
waves that shimmer with their laughter,
the lights of ships dispersed like fantasy
across all the black hollows of the mind,
all the siren songs and hauntings
that drive compulsions in the face of stars.

A mist soft as shadow.
The music of the drowned, that entrances
those lost on cold decks, stranded between their own breath
and the breathing of the sea.

It's then that good men with warmth in their hearts
and heat in their veins, find themselves lured
to flimsy railings, seduced by ancient songs
and the mystery of ages, plummet
silently down the sides of ships,
into the mist, into the sea
that hymns in endless cycles
of death, of life, of transformation,
time's flow and the sea's flow that will carry them
back to the night where the world began.

Iron Cove

Walk the path beside the bay,
the mist rising, the shadow of a boat
passing with throbs across the quiet water
and the morning beginning to open
into sunlight and warmth.

The path winds through groves of trees.
The launch continues its straight course
from point to point, while I twist between parks,
bushes and fences, taking the longer track.

I watch the boat disappear around the headland.
Its silver wake shimmers, vanishes,
as the morning sun smooths the day with its vision
of neatness, order, predictability.

On the distant side of the cove, stacked on
the uncertain shore, red suburban roofs,
like a jigsaw puzzle, started but not complete,
and the main road stressed with traffic,

fluid monotony, featureless and flat.
Joggers and walkers follow routine paths
and cross only on the zebra crossings.
From the jumble there to trees and shade here

before the sun begins to prise apart
the morning into heat and noise and glare.

Effects of Fog

Camille Pissarro, *L'Île Lacroix, Rouen*, Philadelphia Museum of Art, 1888

A river flows from the sky
and the sky's a mirror
of white plates –
the effects of fog.

Pilots flying alone at night
confuse the sky and sea,
report strange lights that hover
above and parallel –
their own lights
reflected from wave caps
like mirrors.
They lumber unknowing, upside-down,
confused by height.
Subtract away infinity,
they disappear into horizontals,
crash when the sky
suddenly turns to sea.

Trust your instruments not your instincts.

Verticals confuse horizons here.
A row of poplars
could be poles marking the channel.
A chimney stack and smoke
appear taller, shimmer
where they shouldn't be.

The mast of a barge
could be one light pole
or another poplar
in a row of seven
and the barge a black reflection,
an edge between plates of white,
confusion of sky and light.
A lone figure in a dinghy
glides among reflected light,

stands to look about –
trusts his instincts
looks at the sea,
remains black
searching for white.

Barangaroo

Hundreds of saplings staked against the wind.
Blond sandstone blocks. Paths and steps that describe
the old shoreline. Darling Harbour below
the legs of skyscrapers, terraces, flights
of steps to the lawn, the centre of the headland
and all the footways leading down to water.

Fifty years ago I first came here,
walking north along Hickson Road and saw
the distant funnel, a passenger ship,
above the wharf sheds. I searched and found her –
Tjiluwah, only nine thousand tons, but a liner
and to me magical. I watched entranced.

Two hundred and sixty passengers, less
than a modern Airbus, sailing in luxury
north to Djakarta, Manila, Hong Kong.
I went on board and hovered in the buzzing crowd.
Today there are rocks where the wharf had been
and paths where the wharf sheds stood.

And *Tjiluwah* was sold, scrapped years ago,
a victim of early jumbos and jets.
I watch the harbour, blue as summer,
wrap myself in a coat against the wind,
cold, southerly. I compare then with now.
The park will be lovely when the trees grow.

Macdonaldtown Station, 7 p.m.

A thin and insecure
peninsular of light.
I hover here alone
exposed by hollowness
and cold,
a ringing space,
monster rivers
sliding through
gusts and showers
of city night.

The Illawarra's
torrent of steel
curves away to Erskineville,
railway beacons tracking south,
river reaches,
narrows of lines funnelled
into cataracts of dark
and swept
from the world's crater,
its valleys sinking
into night, winds
thrown at my face.

An empty drum of air
beats a rhythm-like machine.
From Alexandria, St Peters come
lights along the rim,
a bowl of space
dissolving into nothing
and the humming there
like hollow workshops
streaming from the sky.

Behind,
just metres from my nervous feet
the Western Line's
great rolling Mississippi
surges like the planet.
Tracks and stanchion's
vibrating river bed,
the trunks of trees
and platforms silently
roll like rockfall
in its wake.

From Redfern
in the eerie dark,
creep on
the pinprick
marker lights of trains
approaching in the signalled night,
swelling slowly
from the world of life.
Syncopated dragons
unfolding coil on coil,
nose towards this station,
clatter over points,
then switched disdainfully away
billow past,
their silver thighs lurching
into speed, cascade
like eels, pane on pane
passing yellow,
articulated light,
ferries steaming homewards
from the harbour night.

I stand
alone and cold,
shivering in the wind
as the world
just ebbs away
and the trains
stamp like rivers
through the night.

An Old Photo

In plain black and white,
an elegant, important ship,
snapped from the heights
of the cliffs astern of it,

steams outward bound from Queenstown.
The vast unsettled immensity
of the darkening sea and sky
is cut, inevitably

from all the published prints
as simply quite irrelevant
to the construction of the central image.
As if this small event

did not end with finality
the strength of the nineteenth century's
mad pride in its own technology,
like a knife used in surgery.

That steel can be cut by ice
can be a cause of moral panic:
the last known photograph
of RMS *Titanic.*

The Red Hat

William Frater, 1937, The National Gallery of Victoria

A white dress, a cream jacket,
a young woman, hands on hips, seated, yes,
but leaning forward – her pale skin,
dark eyes and neat black hair, face aslant,
turned towards the light but her eyes
are searching yours.

The red hat dominates her face,
a flow in bold slashed across the forehead,
dipping almost to cover her right eye,
a sinuous flow of soft, of velvet,
a curve and dome and slope of red.

Lina Bryant, twenty-eight,
assertive, determined and the red hat,
cherry red that flames from monochrome,
cherry lips and cherry scarf,
the red of luxury,
temptation, death.

You wore your own red hat for me,
playing at a gangster's moll
as I'd asked you to,
mouthing tough, spitting the words.
Dark eyes, black cascades of hair,
your eyes were searching mine.
You wore black stockings and gloves,
as I'd asked you to,
high heels, nothing else.

A famous painting, an antique hat,
Lina died at sixty-one,
and you wearing a red hat for me,
naked in a moment of almost
make-believe, almost truth.

I'd Never Worked With Glamour

for Caroline Byrne

Sorry, all I did
was ogle your legs –
short skirts, a model's
tools of trade I guess
and no one's young forever
though you continue to be
in ways you never knew
or wanted.

The occasional corridor smile,
greetings as we passed.
I hardly knew your name
or what you did.
You radiated poise –
confidence in the direction
life was taking you.

And now you're gone eleven years.
Hurled to death, they say,
because of secrets
you were unlucky to know,
the men
you were unlucky to love.

A long way – Clarence Street
to the rocks and darkness
at The Gap.

There's money, power and fear,
work and pleasure.
There's beauty and there's death.

Forty Years Ago

Aged fourteen,
I took the harbour road
under the beckoning arch
and explored the finger wharves
around Walsh Bay.

Dodged wharfies,
trucks and customs guards
to ogle and admire
docked and derricked cargo liners,
their house colours and funnels
blatant as centrefolds,
Red Funnel, Blue Star,
Wilhelm Wilhelmsen
and sometimes, quietly
just snuck on board.

Discovered once
Shaw Savill's famous
Northern Star, laid-up,
cold-metal and abandoned,
twenty-four thousand tons
of ocean liner
and not a soul to stop me.
I climbed her main and promenades,
strange as a fallen town.

I explored her every inch
from bridge to engine room,
walked deserted corridors,
the empty public rooms,
and with an eerie wind
prowled her decks
and could have stolen her
if I'd known how.

Months later
she sailed for Hong Kong
and cut up for scrap.
She was twelve years old.

Last night I walked
my wife of thirty years
under the Harbour Bridge,
the Wharf Theatre,
Number Five Walsh Bay
and dodging taxis,
traffic, crowds
enjoyed a play
where the old cargo liners
had loaded and discharged
the world.

Apartments, restaurants
and million-dollar views.
No ships at all.

Camperdown Park

Dolls' box houses
and terraces in rows
stand in silent order,
alert to a view
of water.

Breakwaters of factories.
Pools of green darkness,
the deep watchers –
bandstand, the bowling club
and quiet lagoons of trees
like archipelagos
lost in the roaring dusk.

The flight paths
and landing lights of jets
beating home against the tide
and the terrible torrent
of the major road.

This landfall
only the drowning
or the aimless
could ever know.

For You

For you I'd write
the perfect poem,
simple words of power,

images of bone,
chiselled stone,
polished wood.

I'd write it for you
If I could.

About a Song

The audience wild with rhythm,
stomped to the beat of revolution,
clapped to the images of armies,
the infantry of insurrection.
Twenty-fifth song on the programme,
encore to power and decay,
the unstoppable pulse of marching feet.
He seized his listeners like a bell.

Eisenhower's push into central Germany,
the Eighth Army, seventy years later
in the arena of the concert hall.
Sing the beauty of invasion.
Sing the neoliberals of addiction
and the entrepreneurs of fake.

Here our stalemate of peace and affluence,
we're all consumers of the tawdry.
We're all prisoners of boredom now.
The fascists all wear business suits
and corporations enslave the poor,
the monkeys and their plywood violins.
An anthem for the oppressed and beaten.
The servants and the lowly
and the refugees from power.

And moving through the station
commandos of the shuffling feet,
the regiments of resistance
in the chain-gang uniforms of war.
We sing the battle hymns of revolution
with the Emperor of Cool.
First we take the middle classes,
then we take Berlin…

Not Forgotten

'We first came out on the *Otranto*.'
Magic words. The old Orient liner.
built 1925, scrapped 1957.
Sister to four other ships, only she
and *Orontes* survived the war.

Just her name summons a lost world:
my childhood and the years just before my birth –
the Great Depression, World War Two,
my father's youth and the post-war reconstruction,
I now realise, I was born into.

Discovering my childhood world, ferry trips
into the city, ships at Walsh Bay,
P&O and Orient liners at Pyrmont
and the Quay, corn-coloured, huge funnels.
Otranto scrapped too soon for me to see,

but her image lingered in the books
my father bought for me, two-funnelled,
old fashioned black hull, unlike more modern
liners – *Oronsay, Orcades, Orsova*,
but romantic with age and history,
emblem of a more stately world.

Now I know someone who sailed on her,
a little girl then, from England, an early
post-war immigrant. I was still a boy.
The past, lingers, not forgotten,
ghosts of my childhood in books and memory,
in the passing remarks of others.

Full Moon at Terrigal

The full moon
stands above the sea
and slips her silver gown
away from her shoulders,
lays it like a path
of brilliant marble,
delicate and bright
across the waves, the beach,
the rocks, towards the seventh floor,
our hotel room
and looks down,
flagrant, haughty, nude.

The lighthouse swings
its lesser beam.
Ships anchored off the coast
are merely points of light
lifting the horizon.

The house lights
arc along the beach
like shells
abandoned by the tide.

Later, rising higher, bolder,
the naked moon
has thrown a white carpet of flowers,
a sheen of glamorous ice,
wide across the bay
and the sea shimmers back
like an audience
held spellbound
in her huge, glittering eye.

Essence

Unfair yes –
the meagre, tritest words
insinuate memory
and power
to the crystal punch
of music.

Poets
scratch their words of glass –
no pedal-steel or bass guitars,
no backing vocals
for the words
of merest ink.

We smear the lonely page
with syllables
that burn the soul
like violins,
sear the heart
like cellos.

I live.
I love you.
I'm growing old.

On the Edge

July, the darkest, coldest month.
The sign of Cancer. Those born
under the sign of the crab.

Hard shells may seem
impenetrable but there's always
softness underneath.

Pincers may be claws that leave
nasty wounds but only if
provoked. Rarely aggressive.

Step sideways if cornered. Approach
from odd angles. May grow uncertain
of the dark, ambivalent towards the cold,

betray the ambiguity
of their birth, liminal. There the land
and here the sea, then, now.

Fire at Sea

There are worse things than fire at sea,
he said, but not many.

A shifting dump of coking coal
stews like an angry heart
dropped in the forward hold.
Spillage from old cargoes
fractured into pressure, stress
and overloads from days in port,
holidays at home. The gaps
she should have filled,
sparks from friction, yaws
and rolls and stress at sea.
A woman's small pettiness,
rubbing on a man's greater, louder pettiness
and the slow smoulder
steaming into anger.

Smoke hollows from your load.
Intolerance, irritation under
a vicious cross sea's thud and chop.
Ignition's hellfire shudders up,
coal-fed furnace shots, the ship,
your shipmates and your marriage is
already doomed to loss.
Throw a mug of coffee at your wife
and marriage sinks like keel-break.

Direct the fire hose, nozzles
metalled hot to melting,
the weight of water pumped below
pushes down her head,
heat melting hatch covers,
black molasses at your feet
and in your face tons of coal
in slow eruption crack like doomsday.
She's splintered, broken-backed,
she spits and snaps away,
she's gone beneath your feet.

And son, you're kicking naked
in the lonely sea, your life jacket's
burned to mush, the nearest coast's
drifted leagues off course
more than a dream away, shipping lanes
and rescue God knows where
and mate, just look around,
there's nothing but the endless
hissing sea and the boiling of endless waves.

There are worse things than fire at sea.
The worst of them, he said, is guilt
seers through your heart.
3 a.m. lies sulking on your bunk,
devour real crime and stories for the blood
and thinking how to strangle
any total stranger
or your wife.

Swans

The wild ducks
fuss and fidget
down from the unknown sky,
drift like soft,
high-necked galleons
on the grey river.

Christmas has come again,
another year:

We've flown
the unknown skies
and now the grey river
carries us like swans.

There's No Script

A recurring dream or nightmare, backstage
in a theatre during a play, in costume,
made up, and you're told to go on, the star
is sick, but you've never seen or read the play,
have no idea what it's about and know
absolutely no lines whatsoever.

Just go on, ad-lib, make it up, they say.
You do and the dream ends. It always ends.

The perfect metaphor for life: no script.
You can't predict. You don't know. Then it ends.

Dance of the Knights

from Prokofiev's ballet score *Romeo and Juliet*

The 'undanceable' ballet
lingered in the concert hall for years,
then fifteen curtain calls for the Kirov dancers
lost in the hell of death and war.

At the Capulets' feast,
teenage Juliet, silent, awed,
by the dance of the arrogant toughs.
Inevitably the pulse

of menace and fear – the music's
martial, strident, harsh.
The march of the gangs and Capulets
and Tybalt claims the floor.

Where the sun shines the brightest
the deepest shadows lurk.
In the middle of the feast
the death squad's training.

After the secret wedding
brawling in the street
and Mercutio bleeds to death:
'A plague on both your houses!'

In the midst of life,
in the midst of joy,
something marching towards you,
determined, dark, with burning steps.

Water at Your Feet

The harbour's a blue octopus –
its arms reaching everything.
Look across its width, a man-made cliff,
the coal-loader on Ball's Head Bay,
a green wilderness and clock-work towers
that rise on the far shore and float there on its coil.
But here the water glitters blue,
inserts itself into the ends of streets.

This peninsula, its small terrace houses,
huddled in stone and brick, avoid the tight,
liquid tentacles that clutch at their hearts,
powerful the siren song of flow.
Small boats reply with a knocking
and tinkling of their rig, writhe
in the wind – they rise and fall as if
to twist from their ropes and moorings.

Entranced by the love-songs of waves,
you scuttle between tidelines and the shore,
the moon's sweet gravity builds within you,
a flux of passion and desire, the ebb
that leaves you exhausted, empty as the dawn,
the swing of tides that abandon you naked, dazed.
Emerge rarely onto hard land,
move occasionally towards the light,
retreat to shelter in shadows and rocks,
safe from the pull of the moon, the fist of the sun.

Overwhelming, the waves wild as storms
that build and ebb in your heart,
supple as the swells of the sea, the force
of tides in your bloodstream, its yearning
and mood swings, its mad dance with the moon.

Yet the harbour's as calm as the morning,
reflects the sparkle of a cloudless day
in deep inlets, its inroads into
suburbs that appear merely tranquil.
As always, the land's slow wrestling against
erosion and churn, historic, secret
its immersion deep in rocks and soil,
imminent as the fear of rising water.

In this park, domestic, tidy,
the songs are immense as the world.
Hold to the wooden bench, stare across the harbour,
try to ignore the lure of sunlight and blue.
Think of home, turn your back, walk away
along a street of terraces tangled
safely stone on stone and brick against brick
while the water coils and drives at your feet.

The Lost Child

The full moon rising
mysterious, a searchlight
against the black edge
of ridge, directs its full beam
into our windows
as if seeking the lost home
it once left, and yearns
to return.

Its birth in Hadean night.
The dead planet Theia struck the Earth,
that alien world shattered
into rock and asteroids, now
endlessly cascading between
Mars and Jupiter,
peeled the soft Earth
of its crust, debris in darkness
coalescing into the moon,
swirled forever in orbit
around its old planet-womb,
eternally watching us,
eternally searching
in the emptiness of space,
still tugging the tides to itself,
reflecting the sun's light
in constant reminder
of our lost child
calling to its home,
calling to us
from the high ridge
east of where we are.

Talking to Winter

after Osip Mandelstam

Don't attempt to ignore the city in winter,
wide-open in the grip of its own death.
Respond to the closed door's drunken bellow,
your world crumpled into keys and locks.

Listen to the backstreets barking with mad hymns,
Bibles sodden in gin, twisted lanes where addicts
scurry into corners and their coiled dealers
push them onto the street again.

Talk to tattoos, talk to the vandal,
talk in the rust-streaked waterworks of ice,
in air that's dead, green and crazed with absinthe,
where fevered crows explode with punches.

All you can do is speak to winter,
its wickerworks of frozen wood and the songs
of the ambulance, the raincoat-shielded
whispers spined on narrow back staircases.

Slow Train Coming

for Morrie Egan, died 25 February 2007

A slow train coming , black locomotive.
Its headlight-eye snouts through canyon curves.
It snorts the grades, heaves its dead-weight clockwork.
A midnight crab of steam and steel.

Piston rods revolve and hiss, slow valves,
the lurch and beat of cogs, fat-boilered slug
that leans against the sun, blackens the day.
A long night of furnace fumes, smoke and ash.

A slow train coming, black locomotive,
fire-grates in a tunnel drilled through dark,
Fire-dank crawls from its soot-stained lair,
heaves itself closer, is coming, is coming here.

Three Studies for the Temeraire

Cy Twombly, 1988, the Art Gallery of NSW

No sound, only the mist.
Oars muffled in rowlocks.
Pistons slide with the hiss
of steam and the beat
of paddles somewhere in the mist.
Black ships and reflections.
Water drips from decks
and in their wake shapes slop
in a white world, somewhere
between dreams and death.

Perhaps keels and masts
could be a memory of breath,
or a slow history of dreams.
Mist runs through the mind, shapes
through fingers. Shouts swim into air.

Red on brown rust
dripping from hulls.
Not the red of bright blood
nor the purple of drowned men's lips,
all bleached by seasons rotting of sunlight
like abstracts of the past,
the mythology of water.
The past's a voyage.
The present's merely mist
and the future's here like a bone.

Broadway in the Rain

It was dusk and it was raining.
The roadway glowed with odd reflections
of damp, the glare of the city.
You led me down the hill towards
Glebe. I wasn't sure where you were taking me.
The gutters overflowed and we stepped
across puddles. Your dress was splashed
by a car. Our umbrellas kept knocking
as our own dry bubbles of air
kept us apart and I couldn't
reach your hand.

I hadn't walked down there for years.
New buildings had risen on either side.
Old Broadway felt as alien
and strange as highways to the moon.
You led me to a new restaurant
you'd seen and liked and booked for us.

The strangeness vanished as we sat,
ordered, shared our thoughts, our feelings
and our lives. I lost myself again
in the comfort of you. I held your hand.

When we left, it was still raining
but gently now like whispering words
we'd confided in the night.
We kissed under your umbrella.
I led you to your friend's waiting car.
I waved in the warm rain as you drove
into the bright, welcoming,
familiar street.

A Whitby Bark

The *Earl of Pembroke* glides out of harbour.
Beneath the headland, the northern breakwater
points its long arm into the North Sea,
while the southern closes like a hook
as if barring her return. She sets
full sail on a welcoming sea
and steers towards Newcastle to load
two hundred tons of coal, then the long beat
southwards, the twisting reaches of the Thames
and the coal berths at Wapping Old Stairs.

She is sold and renamed. Her new owners take her
across the Atlantic, around Cape Horn
to Tahiti and the South Seas. She will
circumnavigate New Zealand, sail the east coast
of New Holland and penetrate Torres Strait.

She will transport troops to
The American War of Independence
and end her days as a wreck, the blockade
across Newport Harbour, where she still lies.

She never returns to Whitby
where she was built. Her new owners
the British Admiralty. Her new name
Endeavour.

Faces

Look up the ridge in daylight
there's nothing there.
Look up the ridge in darkness,
one small light, high, near the road.

Every night it's there.
Behind the ridge the moon
rises like a face
so anxious to illuminate

the Earth that it borrows light
from the distant sun,
reflects it and smiles.
But the light on the ridge

is tiny and doesn't smile.
Whose face does it reflect?
What obscure planet or star,
street light or house light?

Someone is there, high on the ridge
and the light guides them home
and makes sense of the darkness
when there is no moon for any of us.

And Sunrise Brings

A mad dash through an iceberg haunted night,
no moon, all steam diverted from heating
to force the ship's engines into full speed,
darkness crumpled by drifting ice,
unseen, prowling, the bergs marked merely
by a green sheen, water lapping
their silent bases, a double lookout stressed
to hail at the slightest sign of danger,

the helm swung three times to avoid
cold catastrophe and the radio
intent on any call, assistance, hope,
but the last was two hours ago.
They'd heard nothing since.

Flat, endless sea, stretching into morning
as the cold sun rises, a spectacle of ice
and water, broken into frozen daylight.
Gaze at an awestruck world,
ice castles, ship-killing towers,
magnificent in symmetry and silence.
To the north, a wall of white, unbroken
to the horizon and at fourteen knots
they'd hurtled blindly into this frozen crucible.

Two boats, one towed by the other,
almost full but still space for others,
wounded creatures crawling towards safety
as if abandoned here by something huge.
Survivors huddled there in shock,
nightwear, evening gowns, life jackets,
some children and one officer in charge,
their fingers too numb to grasp the ladders.
Eased on board, blankets, warmth at last,
they stumble below into comfort and heat.

One question, beyond imagination, but asked
of the first ice wraith brave enough to grab
a ladder, the first of mere seven hundred
to step on board, the purser of Carpathia,
in a voice that wavered, breathless with disbelief,
'But where… Where is *Titanic*?'

Morning Steam

Departure. Valve gear drops to full forward,
warning whistles and blasts from cylinders,
billows of steam that swallow the engine
in storm clouds, in showers of mist and vapour.

A roar of clean superheat escaping
under pressure, the first cough of exhaust
from her funnel, wheels turn, a second blast,
rods and drivers starting into motion,

she edges forward, hesitant, cautious,
draped in cascades, silk screens that camouflage,
movement behind a mass of spreading white,
curtains that swell into a thin steam-haze.

She noses slowly into clearer air,
draws breath and beats with growing confidence,
drags her train into motion, lifts her burden
through the rain and the steam and the smoke.

Carriages slide behind her, draw away
into the morning and, for the watchers left
as the crowds disperse, smells of coal smoke,
an empty station and the damp of cooling steam.

The Way to Work

Once more I take
the morning train
to the city again,
bored by familiar landscapes,
inevitably the stations
always look the same.

Commuters ride the metro
from the Gare d'Austerlitz
or catch the Bus One Hundred
to cross Potsdamer Platz.
They walk to join the morning crowds
who stroll in the Plaza Mayor.

I've caught the express
at Waterloo, the tube at Piccadilly,
stepped from the train in the Gare du Nord,
wandered Alexanderplatz
and walked home the via Cavour…

747s outward bound
shake the suburb again,
seconds after take-off,
they roar across my morning
like missiles to the moon
while this train rattles out of Stanmore
and stops at Newtown soon.

The Song

Your grown-up children both
think you're a staid old thing.
You don't drink, don't eat meat,
don't sing.

You look severe, learned, determined,
you're always at work or reading.
That's what they think.

But I've seen you dance wildly
like a twelve-year-old,
joke and giggle, pleased or excited.
You hurl away inhibitions,
whirl into life like a carnival,
relishing the pleasure.

Yes, I love your darkness, your mystery,
but more, I love the little girl
who's playing hide and seek
with me, behind your smile.

And when you laugh
with helpless glee,
in a torrent of mirth and banter
I'm brave and young and strong.
That's what you do for me.

Behind the serious woman,
the child,
behind the child,
the song.

So long, Marianne

The beach at Hydra, 1960.
An old photo.
Three giants of
language and life.

This man captured
how it felt to be young
in the suburbs of Melbourne,
the 1920s and '30s,
an Australia still numb
from the catastrophe of war
and the shock, the scars and the horror
of a later conflict.

George Johnston, war correspondent, journalist,
novelist, died of drink and TB
at 58.

This woman,
evoked the exotic,
the Greek islands
and lives of simple people,
sponge divers and their women.
Wrote the bigotry of small minds
in her birthplace, the coastal town,
Kiama, she called Lebanon Bay.
Rebellious teenager,
soldier, lover, mother,
columnist in two cities,

Charmian Clift, took her own life
at forty-six.

That so much younger man,
'the Canadian poet',
sang and wrote elegies to life,
visceral, grim, joyous,
made the 1970s tangible
in images that scald us still,
captured time's march, the rhythm and the loss
in songs of the delicate heart.
Leonard Cohen
died only recently,
loved and famous
at eighty-two.

But the fourth figure,
tall, lithe, beautiful,
almost naked in her bikini,
Marianne Ihlen,
his muse
for one of his most famous songs –
the wistful longing for
an almost golden age.

Despite the fading of years,
she's still young in his words,
as immortal in her own way
as her creator.
She stands beside him smiling,
a goddess in the lost mythology
of time and love.

The Owl

A wet and cold December,
exactly the weather I know you hate
and I can take forever,
(ice-guard me, heat-puppy you)
and global warming's gathering
cyclones, inundations, storms,
and you so far from me
I yearn for you.

Like the placid owl
whose outer calm
belies the turmoil there,
this year my flight's direct
through time and hurricane
to you.

The Road

after an anonymous poem of the 1st or 2nd century CE

Those who left draw even further from us.
Those who come are walking towards us.

Leave the city gate and gaze into distances,
mounds, tombs and tombstones, ancient graves

merging under ploughed fields and further
pine and cypress chopped for firewood and coffins.

Poplars bend in a grief of wind,
laments and sighs flowing from the past.

I long to turn towards my old village,
my old home, but this road
doesn't go anywhere near there.

At the National Maritime Museum

A young mother waits with her daughter,
looks out at Darling Harbour, tells her,
'When Betty and Anna arrive, we'll see
lots of ships and maybe some pirates too.'

I look through the main doors at the sharp bow
of *Vampire* looming over us, the black
silhouette of submarine, flat and low,
a viper, sliding beneath her.

At least, *Vampire*'s a handsome ship, sleek
and curved, Daring class, big-gunned destroyer,
but today the sub fills me with horror.
I've descended into her, shuffled her length

and clawed between hatches, claustrophobic,
a spider in machinery. I felt
stunted, dirty in my morality,
glad to scramble out, regain the clean air.

Like people, there are many types of ship
I hope the little girl never meets.
How many children drowned in *Titanic*?
Pirates, more than enough in any life.

Broadway to Balfour Street

There are certain places that sing
the resonance of time and memory.
For years I taught in the classrooms
at the back of the old building,

watched the great yellow jaws tear apart
the factory across Kensington Street,
the tin sheds, the brick warehouses
reduced to piles of rubble, then

to nothing, their wreckage trucked away.
In the distance old jacarandas bloomed
regardless of consequence and loss.

Today I visit what was then destroyed:
melodies of verdant gardens, the tunes
of running water, new glass and silver
tiers of apartment blocks, a shopping centre,
the music of a modern world.

From the third storey I look out
over the park towards the street,
the old house where I first met you
and kept meeting you for a decade, more.

From here I cannot see your street, hidden
by suburban clutter, nor find
the windows I'd previously looked out
at the old world shuddering with collapse

to build the new. It's drizzling and cool,
the sky overcast and grey, beautiful.
Jacarandas pulsate with their purple flowers,
portents of a new summer gathering.

The historic, central building still waits
for restoration. The jacarandas
blaze and the park and the buildings, my heart,
sing to the future but also the past.

Liminal

Departure of the Orient – Circular Quay,
Charles Conder, 1888, Art Gallery of NSW, Sydney

A wet and overcast, grey-day,
the eye drawn to long walls of shoreline
that zig and zag from the brown-hulled liner
easing itself from a far wharf
in a mist of uncertain smoke,
her bow and hull the only curves
against sharp diagonals of foreground –
the *Orient* heaving into life.

Shape and colour build a flatness of water,
where only steam launches glide like beetles
across flat reflections of rain and cloud
to a flat plaza where black crowds gather,
watch black funnels and a red waterline.

Wide dresses, black suits, overcoats,
all black, only the two red umbrellas
huddled into downpour. Crowds still meander
the length of wharf and wharf shed,
mill and chatter, perhaps a last wave,
a quiet tear, farewells and rain.

The verticals of masts and funnels,
the departing liner, blank warehouse walls
that guard the end of the vista. Your vision
too zigzags into brown distance, collides
with the *Orient* at an odd angle
that disrupts straight lines. She rejects the wharf
and shore, begins her voyage into murk
down harbour, a chaos of sea and world.

Whatever Remains

I went back to the place
I'd met you, where I kept meeting you
for years.

It hadn't changed. It was as if
I'd never left. I felt
instantly at home.

I kept thinking of you
but didn't conjure you there.
No ghosts appeared.

I didn't detect your perfume
nor perceive your face.
I couldn't imagine your voice.

The building remains
as it always remains.
We come and go,

go…pass into memory.
There are no ghosts.
All that happens is now.

Acknowledgements

Selected poems appeared in the following Ginninderra Press Pocket Poet chapbooks:

Play it Louder: 'Sunlight and Violins', 'Play it Louder', 'Neil Young Sings "like a Hurricane"', 'Cello Concerto', 'About a Song', 'Essence' and 'Dance of the Knights'

Safe Harbour: 'Down Harbour', 'Iron Cove', 'Barangaroo', 'Forty Years Ago', 'Water at Your Feet' and 'At the National Maritime Museum'

Unexpected Harmony: 'McKenzie's Farm, 1885', 'Camperdown Park' and 'The Way to Work'

Unknown Edges: 'Speak Body, Speak Mind', 'Look Below the Surface' and 'On Lines By Clive James'

Sydney Central: 'Central Railway, 8 a.m.', 'Railway Square', 'Macdonaldtown Station, 7 p.m.' and 'Slow Train Coming'.

Putting to Sea: 'Putting to Sea', 'The Graveyard Watch', 'An Old Photo', 'Fire at Sea' and 'Three Studies for the Temeraire'

Swans: 'The Kiss', 'Swans' and 'The Song'

Dreams of Butterflies: 'Outward Bound the Moon', 'I'd Never Worked With", 'Broadway in the Rain', 'The Owl', 'Broadway to Balfour' and 'Whatever Remains'

Visions: 'The Red Hat' and 'Effects of Fog'

Mischief Eyes: 'For You'

Red Roses: 'Full Moon at Terrigal'

Under Pressure: 'There's No Script' and 'On the Edge'

Speak to Winter: 'Talking to Winter'

Mist and the Rose: 'The Road' and 'The Lost Child'

Poet and the Painter: 'Liminal'

Other selected poems appeared in the following Picaro Poets chapbooks:

This Here and Now: 'Winter's Child', 'A Journey Home', 'So Long Marianne', 'A Whitby Bark', 'Faces', 'And Sunrise Brings' and 'Morning Steam'
Invisible Strings: 'Smoke at Midday'
Around the Table: 'In Her Care'
In Danger: 'Werewolf'
Breathing in the Moon: 'Not Forgotten' and 'Greyworld'

'Soft Rain' appeared in *The Crow*, June 2022, Ginninderra Press.

www.ingramcontent.com/pod-product-compliance
Lightning Source LLC
Chambersburg PA
CBHW070944080526
44587CB00015B/2215